*S*INGLENESS

A Life Grounded in Love

*10 studies
for individuals or groups*

Ruth Goring

With Notes for Leaders

ivp

InterVarsity Press
Downers Grove, Illinois

InterVarsity Press
P.O. Box 1400, Downers Grove, IL 60515-1426
World Wide Web: www.ivpress.com
E-mail: mail@ivpress.com

InterVarsity Press® is the book-publishing division of InterVarsity Christian Fellowship/USA®, a student movement active on campus at hundreds of universities, colleges and schools of nursing in the United States of America, and a member movement of the International Fellowship of Evangelical Students. For information about local and regional activities, write Public Relations Dept., InterVarsity Christian Fellowship/USA, 6400 Schroeder Rd., P.O. Box 7895, Madison, WI 53707-7895, or visit the IVCF website at <www.intervarsity.org>.

LifeGuide® is a registered trademark of InterVarsity Christian Fellowship.

All Scripture quotations, unless otherwise indicated, are taken from the Holy Bible, New International Version®. NIV®. *Copyright ©1973, 1978, 1984 by International Bible Society. Used by permission of Zondervan Publishing House. All rights reserved.*

Cover photograph: Dennis Flaherty

ISBN 0-8308-3097-9

Printed in the United States of America ∞

P	18	17	16	15	14	13	12	11	10	9	8	7	6	5	4
Y	17	16	15	14	13	12	11	10	09	08	07	06			

Contents

Getting the Most Out of *Singleness*

Maybe "getting the most out of singleness" is exactly what you want. You love being single—free to travel, to form relationships with lots of different people, to live simply and spend lots of time with God. You are already getting a lot out of singleness; you just want to make sure you don't miss anything. And there are certain needs you have that your married friends seem oblivious to.

On the other hand, maybe you don't think there *is* much to get out of singleness. You're mostly aware of the lacks in your life—not enough intimacy, no sex, no children, no sense of permanence. You may have lost a spouse or a serious romantic relationship and feel devastated by your aloneness.

Many churches seem to give preference to married people in leadership positions, programs and sermon illustrations. However, Scripture articulates clearly God's special interest in people who are single (especially when it is not by their own will). As a struggling single parent you may feel uncomfortable in church among flocks of rosy, well-put-together, seemingly happy intact families. It's not that God doesn't care about them, but in the Bible you will find that God really wants *you* to know of his watchful care and protection of you and your children.

What is God's word, God's heart, for your life in singleness? The studies that follow help you explore that question—whether you are happy in singleness or find it trying. You will be encouraged to listen deeply to God, to identify the gifts your life offers you, to give those gifts away to others, to grow into Christian community that can help satisfy your needs for belonging and strengthen you in times of struggle.

In the studies you will often come upon questions beginning "How would your prayers be different if . . ." or "How would your life be different if . . ." or "How would your Christian community be different if . . ." It's important to *imagine* if our lives are to deepen and grow. Not imagine what it would be like to be married, but how our lives can be fuller and truer and more beautiful now. Because no matter whether our singleness pleases us or we are working hard to end it soon, while we are single we are not just marking time. God's compassion and calling are for us *today*.

Suggestions for Individual Study

1. As you begin each study, pray that God will speak to you through his Word.

2. Read the introduction to the study and respond to the personal reflection question or exercise. This is designed to help you focus on God and on the theme of the study.

3. Each study deals with a particular passage—so that you can delve into the author's meaning in that context. Read and reread the passage to be studied. The questions are written using the language of the New International Version, so you may wish to use that version of the Bible. The New Revised Standard Version is also recommended.

4. This is an inductive Bible study, designed to help you discover for yourself what Scripture is saying. The study includes three types of questions. *Observation* questions ask about the basic facts: who, what, when, where and how. *Interpretation* questions delve into the meaning of the passage. *Application* questions help you discover the implications of the text for growing in Christ. These three keys unlock the treasures of Scripture.

Write your answers to the questions in the spaces provided or in a personal journal. Writing can bring clarity and deeper understanding of yourself and of God's Word.

5. It might be good to have a Bible dictionary handy. Use it to look up any unfamiliar words, names or places.

6. Use the prayer suggestion to guide you in thanking God for what you have learned and to pray about the applications that have come to mind.

7. You may want to go on to the suggestion under "Now or Later," or you may want to use that idea for your next study.

Suggestions for Members of a Group Study

1. Come to the study prepared. Follow the suggestions for individual study mentioned above. You will find that careful preparation will greatly enrich your time spent in group discussion.

2. Be willing to participate in the discussion. The leader of your group will not be lecturing. Instead, he or she will be encouraging the members of the group to discuss what they have learned. The leader will be asking the questions that are found in this guide.

3. Stick to the topic being discussed. Your answers should be based on the verses which are the focus of the discussion and not on outside authorities such as commentaries or speakers. These studies focus on a particular passage of Scripture. Only rarely should you refer to other portions of the Bible. This allows for everyone to participate in in-depth study on equal ground.

4. Be sensitive to the other members of the group. Listen attentively when they describe what they have learned. You may be surprised by their insights! Each question assumes a variety of answers. Many questions do not have "right" answers, particularly questions that aim at meaning or application. Instead the questions push us to explore the passage more thoroughly.

When possible, link what you say to the comments of others. Also, be affirming whenever you can. This will encourage some of the more hesitant members of the group to participate.

5. Be careful not to dominate the discussion. We are sometimes so eager to express our thoughts that we leave too little opportunity for others to respond. By all means participate! But allow others to also.

6. Expect God to teach you through the passage being discussed and through the other members of the group. Pray that you will have an enjoyable and profitable time together, but also that as a result of the study you will find ways that you can take action individually and/or as a group.

7. Remember that anything said in the group is considered confidential and should not be discussed outside the group unless specific permission is given to do so.

8. If you are the group leader, you will find additional suggestions at the back of the guide.

1

Grounded in Love

Ephesians 3:14-21

Who are you? The easiest answer to this question probably has something to do with your occupation. A deeper though more complicated answer has to do with who you belong to—your relationships with God and others.

GROUP DISCUSSION. Around a circle, take turns defining yourselves in terms of your relationships: "I'm Katherine, daughter of Emma and Charlie, sister of Tom and Marie, cousin of Laura, friend of LaTysha, Peter and Gwen, child of God." Include pets if you wish! In reference to God, use any relational term that is most comfortable (other examples: servant, seeker, follower, friend).

PERSONAL REFLECTION. Do you experience God's love readily, or is it mostly an abstraction for you—a nice idea, even a truth, that is hard to lay hold of? Ask God to open you to more of his love today.

The apostle Paul wants us to know God's love as our deepest source of identity. *Read Ephesians 3:14-21.*

---

1. Paul defines our relationship with God by identifying God as "the Father" (v. 14). What does God's fatherhood mean to you doctrinally?

on an emotional level? (Does that relational picture appeal to you, repel you or leave you cold?)

---

2. In verses 16-19 Paul is praying for an inner process to occur. Looking especially at the verbs he uses, describe the movement of that process.

---

3. Does Christ live in us, or do we live in Christ? Explore this paradox.

---

4. How do you see Paul praying us into relationship with the whole Trinity (though he never uses that term)?

5. What divine resources does the prayer appeal to (vv. 16, 20)?

6. Is Paul praying for individuals or for a corporate experience of Christ? Support your answer from the passage.

7. Why do you think Paul breaks out into praise as he concludes his prayer (vv. 20-21)?

8. Pay attention to all the words painting a picture of largeness. In what ways are you tempted to assume the opposite—that God's love is limited, even stingy?

9. Is your sense of identity—the definition of who you are— grounded in Christ's love? Explain.

How is that either helped or hindered by your singleness?

10. How would you be different if the process you explored in question 2 were completed in you?

How would your church or fellowship be different?

---

11. Given what verse 20 says about God's power, how do your prayers need to be stretched?

Use phrases from Paul's prayer to construct your own prayer for deeper rooting in the vast love of Christ.

Now or Later

"'In Him we live and move and have our being' [Acts 17:28]. Consider that you are in God, surrounded and encompassed by God, swimming in God" (Mother Teresa). Take five to fifteen minutes of silence to use these words as a prayer exercise. Afterward, write down how you felt and anything God showed you.

2

God's Presence in Broken Relationships

In the United States, popular culture—including politics and church—glorifies life in families (the emphasis on "family values," the proliferation of programs to attract and serve married couples with children). In many cultures around the world, in fact, singleness is a matter of shame.

GROUP DISCUSSION. Think of one place where you feel welcome as a single and one setting in which your singleness is uncomfortable. What makes for welcome? What makes for discomfort?

PERSONAL REFLECTION. How has your family—parents, siblings, other relatives—responded to your singleness? Talk to God about how that has made things easier or harder for you.

How does God see those who have lost or have never found the primary bond of marriage? What is his heart for them? *Read Psalm 146.*

1. What would you say is the focus and mood of the psalm?

2. Within the framework of praise, the psalmist calls us to consider certain truths. What warning is offered, and why (vv. 3-4)?

3. When is it tempting to lean too heavily on human beings who cannot "save" us?

4. How does the psalmist contrast God with mortal princes (vv. 5-6)?

5. Who do the movers and shakers of our culture usually pay most attention to?

According to verses 7-9, who are the objects of God's particular care?

---

6. Which of the groups in verses 7-9 do you most identify with? Explain. (You may choose more than one.)

---

7. When do you most readily *feel* God's care?

Do these verses reverse your common perception of God's care and favor? Explain.

---

8. How would you pray differently—for yourself and others—if you took seriously this psalm's description of God?

---

9. How might your church or fellowship look different if it took on God's heart for single parents and their children, widows and widowers, and lifelong singles—as well as immigrants, prisoners, the disabled and other groups listed here?

---

10. Describe how it feels to know that God is *intent* on helping you, that you are living under his watchful eye.

Take up the psalmist's call to praise the God who is faithful forever and who watches over you.

Now or Later

Personalize verses 7-9 by writing down how God has cared for you in each of these ways. For example: "The Lord sets prisoners free. When I was paralyzed by fear, God opened a way for me to escape an abusive marriage. The Lord gives sight to the blind. He has opened my eyes to his great love . . ."

3

Space to Love

When my adopted daughter, Claire, came home with me from her Colombian birthplace, she formed a special bond with my sister Mary Beth (nicknamed Mez). When Mez visited us, they giggled at each other's antics, swam together, cuddled in a rocking chair at bedtime. Mez hosted Claire's first overnight stay away from home.

After this favorite aunt got married and gave birth to a son, though, things changed. She didn't have much energy to be silly with her niece. Claire complained wistfully, "Aunt Mez isn't fun anymore!"

GROUP DISCUSSION. Throw out as many perks of the single lifestyle—trivial and substantial—as you can. Be honest about what you like!

PERSONAL REFLECTION. Think of a single mentor, teacher, spiritual director or friend who has been especially important in your life. Were some of the gifts this person gave connected to his or her singleness?

Is there anything intrinsically good in singleness, or is it always a mistake—an inability to attach, the result of a former partner's failure to love or a failure to find "the one"? The apostle Paul, himself a lifelong single, describes both the struggles and the gifts of singleness. *Read 1 Corinthians 7:25-35.*

1. What is Paul's key recommendation to singles?

What exceptions does he suggest (v. 28)?

2. How does Paul describe the urgent situation that prompts this recommendation?

3. What troubles has your singleness spared you?

4. What contrasting or paradoxical behaviors does Paul recommend in verses 29-31?

5. How would a married person "live as if they did not" have a spouse? (Look at the other paradoxes for clues.)

_____

6. What contrast do verses 32-34 draw between married and single people?

_____

7. How would you summarize Paul's concern "for your own good"? (That is, what is he trying to promote in singles' lives?)

_____

8. Have you found that being single does keep you free to focus on the Lord? (Think about your prayer life, attention, lifestyle choices and ministry to others.)

_____

9. What aspects of church life and the wider culture make it hard for singles to follow in Paul's footsteps today?

_____

10. Given the "many troubles in this life," the potential benefits of singleness and your own emotional makeup, would you rather be single or married right now? Explain.

11. Do you have any models in this realm—singles who "live in a right way in undivided devotion to the Lord"? What would you like to learn from them?

Whether your singleness is chosen or not, pray that it will open you to larger devotion to Christ. Thank God for his devotion to you.

Now or Later

In *The Cloister Walk* (New York: Riverhead, 1996, pp. 255, 260, 263) Kathleen Norris offers some Catholic monastics' reflections on lifelong celibacy. Discuss or journal on whether and how these benefits can hold true even for singles whose celibacy is involuntary or temporary:

☐ "To be celibate . . . means first of all being a loving person in a way that frees you to serve others. Otherwise celibacy has no point."

☐ "The object of celibacy is consciousness, . . . taking our unconscious feelings and sexual urges and placing them where we think God wants them. Our goal is to be celibate, conscious, passionate people."

☐ Celibacy serves us by "stretching the ability to love, and particularly, to love non-exclusively," giving others "the gift of passionate attention."

☐ "The fruit of celibacy . . . is hospitality."

4

Jesus &
His Friends

Matthew 26:36-46

We affirm the incarnation as a cornerstone of our Christian belief. But in some ways, deep down, we find it hard to believe that Jesus was really *human*. For example, until he was on the cross he had unbroken communion with the Father—so weren't his human relationships pure "ministry"? Why would he need friends?

GROUP DISCUSSION. Why do *you* need friends? Call out reasons, and have one group member write them down. Go over your list together. How do you evaluate the various reasons?

PERSONAL REFLECTION. Who has been a good friend to you over a period of time? How did your closeness develop? Thank God for the gift of this friendship.

Today's passage shows the lie in the common pious saying "All I need is God." *Read Matthew 26:36-46.*

___

1. Put yourself in the sandals of one of these three disciples. How would it affect you to see Jesus in such distress?

2. How does Jesus divide his followers into two groups (vv. 36-37)?

Why do you think he does this?

3. Why do you think the disciples keep falling asleep?

4. In your own words, summarize Jesus' prayer to the Father.

5. How can his prayer be a model for yours?

6. What does Jesus' prayer reveal about what he was feeling at this time?

7. Why do you think Jesus longed for his close disciples to stay awake with him? (See vv. 38, 40-41, 45-46.)

8. What does it mean to you that in a time of deep suffering, Jesus—the Son of God—needed human friends?

9. How would you like to grow in friendship with Jesus?

in accepting the friendship Jesus offers you?

10. Based on this account, what meaning and value does friendship have in the eyes of God?

11. How would you like to grow in friendship with others?

12. What is God saying to you about "watching with" friends who are suffering?

Talk to Jesus about what is hard about being a real friend to him and to others. Thank him that he stays awake with you.

Now or Later

Though Jesus never married, he was both a son and a brother. Read these passages and consider what that belonging meant for him: Luke 8:19-21 and 9:57-62; John 19:25-27.

5

God's Presence
in Loneliness

Psalm 142

Even when we are involved in a vibrant Christian community, we experience moments and sometimes long periods of isolation. Many of us find loneliness distressing and even shameful. We hate to be alone, especially in crowds where everyone else seems to be part of a couple or a group.

GROUP DISCUSSION. Do you ever go to a movie or eat in a restaurant by yourself? How do you feel about doing it?

PERSONAL REFLECTION. What is hardest for you about being alone? Bring God these memories and fears.

After creating Adam, the Lord said, "It is not good for the man to be alone" (Genesis 2:18). Take that statement as a biblical framework for prayer in loneliness as you launch into this study. *Read Psalm 142.*

1. As you look through the passage, what strong words and phrases do you notice?

2. Notice also the repetition of "cry" (vv. 1, 5, 6). From David's prayer, how would you describe what he is thinking and feeling?

3. How does the psalmist respond to the silence of aloneness (vv. 1-2)?

4. Do you generally try to fill up silence when you are alone? How?

5. How does David describe his situation (vv. 3-4)?

6. When have you experienced life in a similar way?

7. After David's statement of absolute aloneness in verse 4, how does he affirm God's presence in verse 5?

8. What are David's three requests of God?

9. In what ways do you identify with these three requests?

10. Why is being listened to—by God and others—so important?

11. What are the two anticipated results of God's deliverance (v. 7)?

12. How has God redeemed your aloneness?

Have you been ashamed to speak of your loneliness? Cry out to God about it; tell him how hard it is, and claim him as your refuge.

Now or Later

Try being alone *together.* If you are in a group, have each member take the name of another. If you are going through this study on your own, recruit a friend to do this exercise with you. Stay in the same room, or find places to be alone in the building or on its grounds. For as little as ten minutes or as long as an hour, bring the other person's aloneness before God. Pray through Psalm 142 on his or her behalf; ask God to be present, listen, rescue and liberate.

6

Team Works

In some ways the lifestyles of singles in the twenty-first-century West are a historical anomaly. In most other cultures and times, singles lived with their parents or siblings and were thus involved in the economic and social life of an extended household. By comparison, many of us are rootless; our freedom and autonomy sometimes feel like a complete open-endedness.

GROUP DISCUSSION. Who are some of the oldest singles you know? Do you perceive them as well rooted in relationships, or are they mostly disconnected?

PERSONAL REFLECTION. Do you have fears about growing old alone? Speak your fears to God. Ask him for insight and hope through today's Scripture study.

The apostle Paul is often held up as a model single, but that doesn't mean he didn't need relationships. This text reveals how relationally rich his life was. *Read 1 Thessalonians 1:1; 2:1-12.*

1. Notice the repeated use of "we" in this passage. Is this the "royal we" (used as politicians do), or do you think Paul is being literal? Explain your answer.

2. Have you ever noticed how often married people use "we" when speaking about their lives? Give examples.

3. In what contexts do you use "we" to refer to yourself? Think about your living situation, your work, your church involvement.

4. In chapter 2 Paul, Silas and Timothy review their relational history with the believers in Thessalonica. What spiritually abusive behaviors did they resist as they presented the good news of Christ?

5. How can teamwork in ministry help guard our motives and prevent abuses?

6. What similes of family relationship does this ministry team use to describe their involvement with the Thessalonians (2:7-8, 9, 11-12)?

7. What does this family language suggest about Paul, Silas and Timothy's relationships with each other as well as with the Thessalonians?

8. What important statement was made by their hard work in self-support (v. 9)?

9. Silas and Timothy were among Paul's long-term partners. Do you have long-term partners in faith and life—people with whom you are interdependent and whose needs condition your decisions about your own life? If so, describe those relationships.

If not, how might God be nudging you to become a partner or teammate to a fellow single?

10. How could your small group, single fellowship or church nurture the deepening of long-term friendships and ministry teamwork?

Thank God for the people who need and depend on you. Pray for growing rootedness in Christian community and freedom from the Western god of autonomy.

Now or Later

Read Romans 16:1-16, 21-23 for further examples of Paul's partnership with friends and relatives, both men and women.

7

Jesus &
Temptation

Being single can be fun, fulfilling, even exhilarating. And the person who has escaped an abusive marriage may experience it simply as relief. But just as marriage is hard, singleness has its own set of vulnerabilities and temptations—some of which are, paradoxically, all the more painful for the healthy person who is fully alive emotionally and physically.

GROUP DISCUSSION. How long have you been single? Count from age twenty-one; if you have been married, count the years before and after your marriage. Has living single grown easier or harder over the years? If you are too young for that question to have much meaning, consider what is easy and hard about singleness *now*.

PERSONAL REFLECTION. What one aspect of singleness has been the greatest source of temptation for you? Confess it to God once again, and tell him that you depend on his help.

Jesus was a lifelong single. But does he *really* understand what we struggle with? *Read Hebrews 2:5-18; 4:14-16.*

1. Having compared Jesus to angels in chapter 1, the author now begins comparing him to other human beings. What is the main point of the verses of Psalm 8 that are quoted in Hebrews 2:6-8?

2. What qualifies Jesus to be "crowned with glory and honor" as the ultimate example of humanity?

3. Have you ever noticed that it is in learning of each other's pain that we let down our guard and begin to trust each other? Why is that?

4. According to 2:10-11, what is the second result (besides Jesus' own glory and exaltation) of Jesus' suffering?

5. What does it mean to you that you are Jesus' sister, Jesus' brother—and that he is not ashamed to call you so?

6. Why do you think "I will put my trust in him," from Isaiah 8:17, is quoted here?

7. How does Jesus' descent into death allow death to be defeated?

8. Do you *experience* Jesus as having flesh and blood, as being like you in every way except sin? Explain.

How would it change your prayers if you understood this more fully (see 4:16)?

9. How is Jesus your high priest, the one who can make atonement?

10. Take a few moments of quiet to consider which of these areas of singleness-struggle you need to bring to Jesus as your brother and high priest.
- ☐ being focused on myself, my own desires and needs
- ☐ an unfulfilled need for companionship and intimacy
- ☐ sexual frustration
- ☐ sexual acting out (for example, premarital sex, pornography)
- ☐ staying detached from long-term commitments in ministry, friendships, other areas
- ☐ other:

How can you bring these struggles into the open in your Christian community and let your fellow singles be real brothers and sisters to you, alongside Jesus?

11. What would a safe place for confession, forgiveness and ongoing encouragement look like?

Silently or aloud, thank Jesus that he fully understands and sympathizes with your pain, failure and loneliness. Confess your sins, and claim the power of his suffering on your behalf.

Now or Later

Sexuality is an area of immense struggle for many Christian singles. People are waiting longer to marry, and many find that the wait is stretching into middle age and appearing permanent. We are also living longer than previous generations, and fewer marriages last. With widely available contraception, the risk of pregnancy looms less large—though sexually transmitted diseases, on the other hand, have proliferated. You may have questions or frustrations about what the Christian teaching "no sex outside of marriage" means for healthy but lonely singles who want to follow Jesus.

The issues need to be discussed honestly; we need to bring our uncertainty, frustration, anger and tears into the light. In your group or with an older, trusted Christian single, read 1 Corinthians 6:12-20, discuss it, and ask what it means for your own life as a sexual being. Tell the truth about your past and present behavior and desires. Seek God's wisdom.

8

Finding
Your Well

Genesis 21:8-21

You could say there are two general categories of single Christians. Some of us have lived in a straight line, making fairly wise decisions, avoiding undue risks, finding ourselves protected from serious harm. Others of us have failed miserably, or have been abused or mistreated, or have had to survive tragedy. What is God's word for those of us whose lives feel bent, splintered, even shattered?

GROUP DISCUSSION. On sheets of plain paper, have each person draw a straight line across the middle, then make a rough map of their life's highs and lows (a graph line connecting spots above and below the median line). Divide into pairs and take turns giving each other a brief summary of your map. Make sure not to disparage each other for "too much" evenness or "too much" up-and-down drama.

PERSONAL REFLECTION. Is your life more straight-line or broken-line? Neither is more valuable; both require God's redemption. Give God your life trajectory, and ask him to redeem every part of it.

Today we consider the story of someone who had very little choice in the course of her broken life. *Read Genesis 21:8-21.*

1. Who are the two sons of Abraham introduced in verses 8-9? Review what you know of their background.

2. Have you, or has someone close to you, been part of a blended family something like the one pictured here? How did the half-siblings or stepsiblings get along?

3. What is Sarah's complaint against Ishmael, and how does she act on it?

4. What is Abraham's response?

What does God tell him to do, and what reassurance does he give?

5. Describe the plight of Hagar and her teenage son as they sit under the bushes in Beersheba.

6. What reassurance does God give Hagar, and what commands?

7. What is God's *immediate* provision for this mother and son?

How does God meet their *long-term* needs?

8. Do you know anyone who has been in a plight like Hagar's?

How do you identify with Hagar? Take time to reflect silently on this question.

9. Has God led you to a "well" in any place of your own suffering—a source of renewal for you and refreshment that you can give to others?

Thank God for meeting you in the deserts of your past. Ask him to hear your cry regarding any thirst, any need, that remains.

Now or Later

Is there a Hagar—someone who has been displaced and ill-treated—in your neighborhood, school or workplace? Pray and consider how you might be part of God's provision for her or him. Remember that God listens to and *hears* our cries; thus your caring should begin with listening, paying attention, to discern what the real needs are. Then give out of the well God has given you.

9

Receiving Life
with Thanksgiving

1 Timothy 4:1—5:2

When I was growing up in the 1960s and early 1970s, I met very few women who did something other than homemaking, secretarial work, teaching or nursing. Since none of these was particularly appealing to me as a lifelong occupation, vocational decision making proved difficult for me. I lacked role models.

As singles, too, we need role models—older singles who have weathered life storms and proved God's faithfulness and who live with delight and abandon.

GROUP DISCUSSION. Do you have such a mentor or role model? Spend a few minutes expressing appreciation for this person's ministry in your life.

PERSONAL REFLECTION. Do you live with delight and abandon—and are you in relationship with people who can help you grow in courage and openness? Talk to God about your desire and your need.

Timothy was blessed to have a long-term mentor with much wisdom to share. *Read 1 Timothy 4:1—5:2.*

---

1. What are the faith-denying errors that Paul wants Timothy to resist (4:1-3)?

---

2. Have you encountered, and perhaps been influenced by, similar false teachings in religious circles? Describe the harm these errors cause.

---

3. How would your life change if you began accepting *everything* God created as good, consecrating each gift with God's word and prayer?

---

4. In the context, what are the "godless myths and old wives' tales" Paul is referring to (v. 7)?

---

5. What does Paul mean by "godliness" here (vv. 7-8)?

6. Paul emphasizes in verses 9 and 10 that we are to put our hope in God. Why then do Paul and Timothy say that they "labor and strive" (v. 10) over this gift of divine grace?

7. List the reminders Paul places before Timothy in verses 11-16.

8. In the midst of these exhortations, how does Paul affirm his son in the faith?

9. Against the context of godliness as Paul framed it earlier, what is he saying about taking care of yourself as you nurture others?

10. If you had a wise mentor like Paul, what would be some of the practical advice he or she would need to offer you along these lines?

11. Verses 1-2 of chapter 5 reflect a theme that has emerged frequently in the course of this study. What hinders the development of such relationships?

12. What one step could you take to live out the "familyness" of the body of Christ?

Receive your own life with thanksgiving, mentioning to God some of the good gifts you are grateful for.

Now or Later

To consider at some length what Jesus' incarnation and death on the cross mean for our life as whole, godly persons, study Colossians 2:6-23.

10

Enlarging Your Tent

Isaiah 54

Do our lives have permanent value? People who are married may readily answer this question by pointing to spouse and children—persons in whom they have invested their lives, who can carry on a legacy. But what if we don't have children, or what if our children have not been blessed to grow up in a stable two-parent home? Can we, will we, still have a legacy?

GROUP DISCUSSION. What is your current home like—efficiency apartment, luxury condo, house with yard? Is it mainly a way station for watching TV and sleeping, or do you feel settled in a homey, hospitable environment? Describe it briefly.

PERSONAL REFLECTION. Where have you been investing most of your time and energy (physical, emotional, mental) over the past few years? Are these tasks and relationships of long-term value, or have you only been marking time?

To consider the long-term meaning of our lives, we need a poem, a song. *Read Isaiah 54.*

---

1. Who is the "barren woman" being addressed in this poem?

---

2. Is barrenness a plight that feels utterly foreign to you, or do you—literally or figuratively—identify with it? Explain.

---

3. Why is the barren woman called to rejoice?

---

4. What concrete action will express her faith in God's promise (v. 2)?

---

5. Summarize the marriage story of verses 4-8.

---

6. How does God name himself here (v. 5)?

7. How could these names and descriptions build the Israelites' hope for their future as a nation?

8. How can they build *your* hope for a meaningful future?

9. What are the images of restored relationship in verses 9-10, and how do they communicate permanence?

10. Translate the poetic promises of verses 11-17. What do they say about beauty?

about fruitfulness?

about safety and protection?

11. Who are the children in the faith—physically or spiritually younger folks—whose nurture you take ongoing responsibility for?

12. Where does the tent of your heart—your life—need to be extended?

Use the images of this poem—healing of barrenness, a widened tent, restoration of intimacy, city walls decorated with jewels, the deflection of attacks—to ask God for a large heart, a fruitful life.

Now or Later

Celebrate the fruitfulness of community by having a meal together. Make it festive with special foods, and encourage each other to bring gifts of poetry, visual art or music. If you are doing this study on your own, invite a few single friends into such a celebration with you.

Leader's Notes

MY GRACE IS SUFFICIENT FOR YOU. (2 COR 12:9)

Leading a Bible discussion can be an enjoyable and rewarding experience. But it can also be *scary*—especially if you've never done it before. If this is your feeling, you're in good company. When God asked Moses to lead the Israelites out of Egypt, he replied, "O Lord, please send someone else to do it"! (Ex 4:13). It was the same with Solomon, Jeremiah and Timothy, but God helped these people in spite of their weaknesses, and he will help you as well.

You don't need to be an expert on the Bible or a trained teacher to lead a Bible discussion. The idea behind these inductive studies is that the leader guides group members to discover for themselves what the Bible has to say. This method of learning will allow group members to remember much more of what is said than a lecture would.

These studies are designed to be led easily. As a matter of fact, the flow of questions through the passage from observation to interpretation to application is so natural that you may feel that the studies lead themselves. This study guide is also flexible. You can use it with a variety of groups—student, professional, neighborhood or church groups. Each study takes forty-five to sixty minutes in a group setting.

There are some important facts to know about group dynamics and encouraging discussion. The suggestions listed below should enable you to effectively and enjoyably fulfill your role as leader.

Preparing for the Study

1. Ask God to help you understand and apply the passage in your own life. Unless this happens, you will not be prepared to lead others. Pray too for the various members of the group. Ask God to open your hearts to the message of his Word and motivate you to action.

2. Read the introduction to the entire guide to get an overview of the entire book and the issues which will be explored.

3. As you begin each study, read and reread the assigned Bible passage to familiarize yourself with it.

4. This study guide is based on the New International Version of the Bible. It will help you and the group if you use this translation as the basis for your study and discussion.

5. Carefully work through each question in the study. Spend time in meditation and reflection as you consider how to respond.

6. Write your thoughts and responses in the space provided in the study guide. This will help you to express your understanding of the passage clearly.

7. It might help to have a Bible dictionary handy. Use it to look up any unfamiliar words, names or places. (For additional help on how to study a passage, see chapter five of *How to Lead a LifeGuide Bible Study*, InterVarsity Press.)

8. Consider how you can apply the Scripture to your life. Remember that the group will follow your lead in responding to the studies. They will not go any deeper than you do.

9. Once you have finished your own study of the passage, familiarize yourself with the leader's notes for the study you are leading. These are designed to help you in several ways. First, they tell you the purpose the study guide author had in mind when writing the study. Take time to think through how the study questions work together to accomplish that purpose. Second, the notes provide you with additional background information or suggestions on group dynamics for various questions. This information can be useful when people have difficulty understanding or answering a question. Third, the leader's notes can alert you to potential problems you may encounter during the study.

10. If you wish to remind yourself of anything mentioned in the leader's notes, make a note to yourself below that question in the study.

Leading the Study

1. Begin the study on time. Open with prayer, asking God to help the group to understand and apply the passage.

2. Be sure that everyone in your group has a study guide. Encourage the group to prepare beforehand for each discussion by reading the introduction to the guide and by working through the questions in the study.

3. At the beginning of your first time together, explain that these studies are meant to be discussions, not lectures. Encourage the members of the group to participate. However, do not put pressure on those who may be hesitant to speak during the first few sessions. You may want to suggest the following guidelines to your group.

☐ Stick to the topic being discussed.

◻ Your responses should be based on the verses which are the focus of the discussion and not on outside authorities such as commentaries or speakers.

◻ These studies focus on a particular passage of Scripture. Only rarely should you refer to other portions of the Bible. This allows for everyone to participate in in-depth study on equal ground.

◻ Anything said in the group is considered confidential and will not be discussed outside the group unless specific permission is given to do so.

◻ We will listen attentively to each other and provide time for each person present to talk.

◻ We will pray for each other.

4. Have a group member read the introduction at the beginning of the discussion.

5. Every session begins with a group discussion question. The question or activity is meant to be used before the passage is read. The question introduces the theme of the study and encourages group members to begin to open up. Encourage as many members as possible to participate, and be ready to get the discussion going with your own response.

This section is designed to reveal where our thoughts or feelings need to be transformed by Scripture. That is why it is especially important not to read the passage before the discussion question is asked. The passage will tend to color the honest reactions people would otherwise give because they are, of course, supposed to think the way the Bible does.

You may want to supplement the group discussion question with an icebreaker to help people to get comfortable. See the community section of *Small Group Idea Book* for more ideas.

You also might want to use the personal reflection question with your group. Either allow a time of silence for people to respond individually or discuss it together.

6. Have a group member (or members if the passage is long) read aloud the passage to be studied. Then give people several minutes to read the passage again silently so that they can take it all in.

7. Question 1 will generally be an overview question designed to briefly survey the passage. Encourage the group to look at the whole passage, but try to avoid getting sidetracked by questions or issues that will be addressed later in the study.

8. As you ask the questions, keep in mind that they are designed to be used just as they are written. You may simply read them aloud. Or you may prefer to express them in your own words.

There may be times when it is appropriate to deviate from the study guide.

For example, a question may have already been answered. If so, move on to the next question. Or someone may raise an important question not covered in the guide. Take time to discuss it, but try to keep the group from going off on tangents.

9. Avoid answering your own questions. If necessary, repeat or rephrase them until they are clearly understood. Or point out something you read in the leader's notes to clarify the context or meaning. An eager group quickly becomes passive and silent if they think the leader will do most of the talking.

10. Don't be afraid of silence. People may need time to think about the question before formulating their answers.

11. Don't be content with just one answer. Ask, "What do the rest of you think?" or "Anything else?" until several people have given answers to the question.

12. Acknowledge all contributions. Try to be affirming whenever possible. Never reject an answer. If it is clearly off-base, ask, "Which verse led you to that conclusion?" or again, "What do the rest of you think?"

13. Don't expect every answer to be addressed to you, even though this will probably happen at first. As group members become more at ease, they will begin to truly interact with each other. This is one sign of healthy discussion.

14. Don't be afraid of controversy. It can be very stimulating. If you don't resolve an issue completely, don't be frustrated. Move on and keep it in mind for later. A subsequent study may solve the problem.

15. Periodically summarize what the group has said about the passage. This helps to draw together the various ideas mentioned and gives continuity to the study. But don't preach.

16. At the end of the Bible discussion you may want to allow group members a time of quiet to work on an idea under "Now or Later." Then discuss what you experienced. Or you may want to encourage group members to work on these ideas between meetings. Give an opportunity during the session for people to talk about what they are learning.

17. Conclude your time together with conversational prayer, adapting the prayer suggestion at the end of the study to your group. Ask for God's help in following through on the commitments you've made.

18. End on time.

Many more suggestions and helps are found in *How to Lead a LifeGuide Bible Study,* which is part of the LifeGuide Bible Study series.

Components of Small Groups

A healthy small group should do more than study the Bible. There are four components to consider as you structure your time together.

Nurture. Small groups help us to grow in our knowledge and love of God. Bible study is the key to making this happen and is the foundation of your small group.

Community. Small groups are a great place to develop deep friendships with other Christians. Allow time for informal interaction before and after each study. Plan activities and games that will help you get to know each other. Spend time having fun together—going on a picnic or cooking dinner together.

Worship and prayer. Your study will be enhanced by spending time praising God together in prayer or song. Pray for each other's needs—and keep track of how God is answering prayer in your group. Ask God to help you to apply what you are learning in your study.

Outreach. Reaching out to others can be a practical way of applying what you are learning, and it will keep your group from becoming self-focused. Host a series of evangelistic discussions for your friends or neighbors. Clean up the yard of an elderly friend. Serve at a soup kitchen together, or spend a day working on a Habitat house.

Many more suggestions and helps in each of these areas are found in *Small Group Idea Book*. Information on building a small group can be found in *Small Group Leaders' Handbook* and *The Big Book on Small Groups* (both from InterVarsity Press). Reading through one of these books would be worth your time.

Study 1. Grounded in Love. Ephesians 3:14-21.

Purpose: To focus on the source of our deepest identity.

Question 1. Jesus suggests one of the implications in Matthew 7:9-11: our heavenly Father can be trusted to give us good gifts. The writer of Hebrews considers another in Hebrews 12:4-13: in our hardships we can sometimes see God's loving parental discipline.

It's important not to assume that fatherhood is a warm concept—for many people it isn't. Encourage honest responses but realize that this may be a very sensitive topic for some.

Question 2. An inner strengthening opens the space for Christ to make his dwelling in us. We put down roots in his love, become securely attached there and learn (grasp) the vast scope of that love in which we live. Then we are filled with God's fullness.

Question 3. Try to avoid the assumption that *heart* means "emotions." In Scripture *heart* means the deepest, truest part of the person, encompassing thoughts, attitudes and moral will as well as feelings.

We put down roots in God's love as Christ dwells in us. Paul's image of a mutual "coming in" echoes Jesus' prayer to the Father in John 17:22-23: "that they may be one as we are one: I in them and you in me."

Question 6. Note that the Greek word we translate "you" in Paul's letters is generally plural—unfortunately not reflected in English translation. He is describing an inner process, yet he apparently wants the church to experience it together (vv. 18, 21).

Question 9. Pain may begin to surface at this point if group members have been able to be honest and vulnerable. What does it say if we have grown in laying hold of Christ's love yet still feel an acute relational lack? Steer people away from facile assurances that "all you need is God" (study four will address this directly). Paul does not say that Christ takes away all our human needs but that Christ is deeply *with* us.

Now or later. Especially if most members of the group are younger singles, they may appreciate reading Albert Y. Hsu's *Singles at the Crossroads: A Fresh Perspective on Christian Singleness* (Downers Grove, Ill.: InterVarsity Press, 1997) as they go through this study. It will help make discussions informed, lively and thoughtful.

Study 2. God's Presence in Broken Relationships. Psalm 146.

Purpose: To be blessed by God's special concern for those who are humanly disconnected.

Question 1. Notice the emphasis on praise in the first and last verses.

Question 2. Encourage group members to restate verse 3's warning in contemporary terms. Who or what are some of the modern "princes" we are tempted to trust?

Question 3. Be sensitive as participants consider this question. The point is not that interdependence is unhealthy; it is that we cannot look to another human being for salvation or ultimate meaning. Also, the psalmist is not condemning "princes" for moral failures in this case, merely reminding us of their mortality.

Question 4. The contrast is multifaceted. Consider the human spirit that "departs" versus God's remaining "faithful forever"; the bodies that "return to the ground" in contrast to the Creator of that same ground; those whose "plans come to nothing" versus the One who made all that is.

Question 6. Remind group members that in the patriarchal culture of biblical times (as in many cultures today), to be fatherless or a widow, and thus without male protection, was to be particularly vulnerable. Certainly God is pictured as befriending the lonely (which would also include the motherless and widowers), but there is special focus on those who are *socially powerless and voiceless,* in need of an advocate.

Question 7. It's normal to feel blessed and cared for when we are not oppressed, harmed or deprived. Yet it is in times of such need, the psalmist says, that God lavishes particular attention on us.

Question 9. Steer discussion away from lapsing into a gripe session—though significant pain may surface that needs to be listened to. Encourage members in a positive direction, to dream of ways the Christian community could reflect God's concerns more faithfully.

Study 3. Space to Love. 1 Corinthians 7:25-35.

Purpose: To consider how our singleness frees us to love others well.

Question 2. The words "crisis" and "time is short" suggest that he believes Christ's return is coming soon. He clearly has a sense of time's significance in the midst of opposition and persecution.

Question 5. This may be maddening for black-and-white thinkers! But Paul is a complex thinker; he qualifies many of his statements and embraces paradox. There is no need to look for one correct answer here. However, it may be helpful to think of some married leaders in the early church. Peter was married, yet he left behind his fishing livelihood to travel with Jesus. We don't know how his wife was supported during that time. Later he was jailed for preaching about Jesus (Acts 4); if he had been thinking only of his family's needs he wouldn't have taken risks like this.

Question 7. The overly scrupulous may try to find some moral argument here. Point them back to verse 28—Paul's concern in this case is *not* sin.

Question 8. It is important to be honest—some group members may *not* believe that singleness has increased their focus on the Lord. Accept their disagreement and acknowledge that Paul is speaking as an older brother here (saying, in effect, "This works for me"), not as having a command from God to enforce singleness.

Question 9. Members will likely be able to think of reasons beyond these: Often churches seem to prefer that their pastors and leaders be married. In the culture at large, autonomy and disconnection from extended family lead to loneliness and lack of community in singles' lives. Chastity is hard amid the sexual hype that surrounds us.

Study 4. Jesus & His Friends. Matthew 26:36-46.

Purpose: To better understand our human need for relationships, in light of Jesus' need.

General note. Jesus is clearly aware that he faces his greatest suffering—the death he had warned his followers to expect (as in Mt 16:21). Whether he knew everything that was to come, at this point and throughout his earthly life, is a matter of some debate among Christians. Some argue that in becoming human the Son "made himself nothing" or "emptied himself" (Phil 2:5-7; see also 2 Cor 8:9) of omniscience as well as other privileges of the Godhead. Clearly he did have prophetic knowledge, but this may have been given to him "as needed" by the Holy Spirit (whose guidance is noted in Lk 4:1, for example).

Question 1. Remind the group of the context—or have a knowledgeable member do so. Jesus was especially close to Peter, James and John. He and the Twelve have just had the Last Supper together; in the course of it Jesus predicted Peter's denial and Judas's betrayal. He also spent a long time opening his heart, revealing more about his intimate relationship with the Father, preparing the disciples for coming hardships and promising them the help of the Holy Spirit.

Question 3. Of course it is late in the night, and they have just drunk wine during the Passover meal. They are also undoubtedly confused and emotionally overwhelmed. Some people readily tune out under such circumstances. You may find it interesting to discuss, though, whether women disciples might have responded differently!

Question 4. Jesus is emotionally honest and does not seem to feel guilty for wishing things could be different.

Question 5. You may want to talk about how feelings of guilt sometimes hinder our honesty with God. Do we believe God needs us to "be nice" and undemanding in our prayer? How can we seek God's will *boldly,* as Jesus does here?

Question 7. Jesus is concerned for their own strengthening as they are about to face his terrible suffering—but his first reason is simply his own sadness. Clearly this account presents a challenge to theologies of God's "impassibility"—the notion from ancient Greek philosophy that God is immune to emotion.

Question 9. John 15:12-15 emphasizes that Jesus has made his disciples friends rather than merely servants carrying out his wishes. You may want to expand this question by asking what it might mean to *stay awake with Jesus.* What grieves God's heart? How might we pay attention to those things rather than tuning out?

Question 12. It is tempting to stay detached from someone in pain, especially when we aren't related by blood or marriage. But even as singles, we need not to rattle around loose in the world but to belong deeply to a few people—to stay awake when they suffer and open up our own sufferings to them, asking for their companionship. This—especially the latter—is hard for self-sufficient people!

Study 5. God's Presence in Loneliness. Psalm 142.

Purpose: To acknowledge the pain of aloneness and find God present in it.

Question 1. Note phrases like "my spirit grows faint within me" (v. 3) and "no refuge" (v. 4).

Question 4. Western cultures, and urban cultures all over the world, provide us with ubiquitous noisemakers to keep silence at bay—television, radio, CD/DVD/tape players. Avoid the simplistic idea that silence is good and sound is bad, but guide the group to consider when filling silence is creative (prayer, music making, speaking truth) and when it is *just* noisemaking.

Question 5. The note introducing this psalm says it comes from "when David was in the cave." This would be the period in which King Saul was trying to kill him, so David was forced into the wilderness, where he moved from place to place, including various caves, to escape Saul's murderous forays. See 1 Samuel 22:1-2 and 24:1-3.

Question 6. Don't assume that group members will identify only with David's emotional aloneness and not his physical vulnerability. If it is a mixed group, the men may need to listen carefully to women's description of the care they must take when they are out alone at night. Perhaps some of them have been assaulted. Of course men may have been physically attacked as well, but they need to understand the constant watchfulness that often goes with being single and female.

Question 7. The group may want to speculate on why "I have no refuge" (v. 4) is immediately contradicted by "You are my refuge" (v. 5). Is he feeling sorry for himself and then reminding himself of the truth? Or is he saying first that he has no *human* refuge and then that there is divine refuge?

"Portion in the land of the living" refers to an inheritance or allotment.

Question 10. One of the terrible things about being isolated is being disregarded ("no one is concerned for me . . . no one cares," v. 4). When we know we are seen and listened to, we are no longer alone. Beyond this, in Scripture God's hearing is connected to God's action in response (see, for example, Ex 3:7-9).

Question 11. David anticipates that when he is set free from his isolation, he will overflow in praise to God. You may want to talk about how this first consequence—praise—leads to the second: others are drawn to the person who acknowledges God's goodness.

Question 12. Catholic thinkers and mystics have long emphasized the value of aloneness. "Thomas Aquinas . . . calls celibacy a vacancy for God. . . . The celibate becomes a living sign of the limits of interpersonal relationships and of the centrality of the inner sanctum that no human being may violate" (Henri J. M. Nouwen, *Clowning in Rome,* rev. ed. [New York: Doubleday/ Image, 2000], pp. 43, 47). Yet monastic celibacy and solitude are set in the context of a committed community. As we saw in study four, desire for human intimacy and companionship is not a sick need but a healthy, God-created condition of our aliveness.

Study 6. Team Works. 1 Thessalonians 1:1; 2:1-12.

Purpose: To examine Paul's model of singleness, which involves living, working and traveling as part of a team.

Question 1. Of course 1:1 is solid evidence for a literal "we." Note that Paul does use "I" when speaking of and for himself alone—for example, Galatians 2:11-14 and Colossians 1:24-29 (though Colossians is sent from both Paul and Timothy).

Use of "we" is evidence of solid connections with others, a sense of identi-fication with and belonging in a partnership or group.

Question 4. An account of this original visit can be found in Acts 17:1-10 (continue in Acts 17:11-15 to see how persecution followed Paul's team out of Thessalonica).

Question 5. Of course working in groups does not automatically prevent abuse of authority or doctrinal error; group members can doubtless think of team-led cults and fellowships whose leaders actually reinforced each other's dishonesty or spiritual abusiveness. You may want to spend a few minutes defining genuine biblical teamwork, in which members of the body hold each other accountable. Paul's confrontation of Peter over his discriminatory behavior is an example (see Gal 2:11-14).

Question 7. Consider how good parents (mothers, v. 7; fathers, vv. 11-12) relate to each other while caring for their children: sharing tasks, communi-cating about each child's needs, enjoying the children together, conferring when there is a difficult problem or a need for discipline. Good parents also show respect and care for each other; this provides their children with a deep sense of security.

Question 8. Paul is not making a blanket statement regarding the superiority of tentmaking (self-support) versus paid ministry. Jesus himself accepted lodging and financial help from various people during the years of his public ministry (for example, Lk 8:1-3; 10:5-8). In some contexts we love best by taking care of our own needs and asking for nothing; in others we love best by accepting help.

Question 9. Encourage participants to think not only of how they partner in their "ministries" (volunteer involvement or paid work in a church or nonprofit organization) but of the orientation of their lives: how they make decisions, where and with whom they live, how they support themselves and spend their money, to whom they are accountable.

Help group members recognize such relationships as gifts: children, god-children, an elderly parent who requires care, a longtime ministry partner or prayer partner, siblings, neighbors who have become like family. You may want to recommend Rodney Clapp's *A Peculiar People* (Downers Grove, Ill.: InterVarsity Press, 1997) for its thoughtful consideration of the body of Christ as the source of our deepest human rootedness.

Study 7. Jesus & Temptation. Hebrews 2:5-18; 4:14-16.

Purpose: To empower us to face temptation with the knowledge that Jesus fully understands.

Question 1. "In their original context, these verses celebrate the exalted position of human beings in God's creation. However, the psalmist speaks in ideal terms, since sin, death and the devil prevent us from exercising dominion in this world as God intended. . . . Complete dominion is promised to the Messiah in Ps. 110:1 and Hebrews takes that text as a clue to the ultimate meaning and application of Ps. 8:4-6. The Son's role is to fulfil the destiny of the human race" (David Peterson, "Hebrews," in *New Bible Commentary,* 21st Century Edition, ed. D. A. Carson et al. [Downers Grove, Ill.: InterVarsity Press, 1994], p. 1327).

Question 4. Be sure people notice that the benefits of Jesus' suffering and death for us include not only following him into glory and holiness but discovering that we are part of the same family.

Question 6. There is no one right answer to this question—but you may want to encourage the group to consider when trust is necessary: when we are vulnerable to danger or threat. As a human being, Jesus was vulnerable on many levels and had to trust the Father as he would not have had he remained in heaven.

Question 9. The high priest in Jewish temple worship had to be morally and even physically perfect (Lev 21). "When the priests received sacrifices and offerings, they signified God's acceptance of the [person bringing the] offering (Lev 1—8). When the priest ate the peace offerings with the offerers, he signified God feasting in fellowship with them. Besides . . . representing God to the people, [the high priest served in] representing the people to God. . . . The most poignant example is the high priest's sprinkling blood on the ark on the Day of Atonement (Lev 16). . . . [Jesus] is the high priest par excellence because he made himself the sacrifice par excellence" ("Priest," in *Dictionary of Biblical Imagery,* ed. Leland Ryken, James C. Wilhoit and Tremper Longman III [Downers Grove, Ill.: InterVarsity Press, 1998], pp. 662-63).

Question 10. Depending on the makeup of your group and the amount of time you've been together, you can either take time for silent reflection and then use the general follow-up or allow people to name the area they want to work on. Consider prayerfully how to create a safe place where people will be heard and loved in the midst of their struggle.

If the group has built good trust by this point, they may have already discussed at least some of these areas of struggle. Note the use of the word *struggle* rather than *temptation,* since some of these express healthy vulnerability rather than brokenness or sin. Since Jesus was *fully* human, for example, we can reverently assume that his five senses were exquisitely attuned to beauty and his sexual longings were powerful. Some unfulfilled desires are healthy, not sick.

Question 11. If you are studying in a group, then you might take the opportunity to discuss how your group can be a safe and accountable place for people. **Now or later.** Helpful books to use in such a discussion include Robbie Castleman, *True Love in a World of False Hope* (Downers Grove, Ill.: InterVarsity Press, 1996), and Russell Willingham, *Breaking Free: Understanding Sexual Addiction and the Healing Power of Jesus* (Downers Grove, Ill.: InterVarsity Press, 1999).

Study 8. Finding Your Well. Genesis 21:8-21.

Purpose: To see a vivid example of God's care for the bereft, mistreated and abandoned.

Question 1. Sarah, unable to conceive a child, had asked Abraham to sleep with her slave Hagar—apparently a common way of dealing with infertility in their ancient Near Eastern culture. Hagar did conceive, but instead of being a docile surrogate mother, she began to put on airs. Sarah treated her badly, and Hagar fled into the desert. There she had her first angelic encounter: an angel prophesied about Ishmael, the son she was carrying in her womb, and told her to return to her mistress. Hagar complied. Ishmael means "God hears" (see Gen 16).

Fourteen years later, the aged Sarah miraculously gave birth to her own prophesied son, Isaac (Gen 21:1-7). This boy was to be the beginning of the offspring of blessing God had promised Abraham long before (Gen 12:2).

Question 2. Interestingly, biblical scholar Catherine Clark Kroeger surmises that Hagar may be the first dark-skinned African woman in the Bible: "There is a good likelihood that she was a black womn captured in Nubia and brought as a slave to Egypt. I suspect that she may have been part of the gift-package which Pharaoh, king of Egypt, gave Abraham in return for his wife, Sarah . . . (Genesis 12:16)" (Catherine Clark Kroeger, "Black Is Blessed: A Study of Black and/or African Women in the Bible," typescript, Christians for Biblical Equality, n.d.).

Question 3. It is not entirely clear whether Ishmael's misbehavior was just common adolescent meanness or something more serious. "Sarah sees the adolescent Ishmael engaging in behavior that threatens the newly weaned Isaac. A Hebrew verb . . . sometimes having sexual and abusive connotations is used to describe the older brother's conduct" (Catherine Clark Kroeger and Nancy Nason-Clark, *No Place for Abuse* [Downers Grove, Ill.: InterVarsity Press, 2001], pp. 96-97).

Question 6. Make sure group members make the connection with Psalm 142 (study five): we pray God to *hear* us, because we know that when God hears, he acts. Hagar's words may also be drawing on the meaning of Ishmael's name (see note 1 in this chapter). She finds out that her cries and Ishmael's have not fallen into an uncaring silence but have lodged in God's heart.

Question 8. Depending on the makeup of your group, you might ask people to discuss how they relate to Hagar, or you might let them reflect silently. It could be an intense question for some, but it is very important for people whose lives have rough edges to see that the Bible is full of God's loving encounters with people like them. In fact, after the words to Eve in Genesis 3, God's encounters with the outcast slave Hagar are the first recorded words of God to a woman in Scripture. Rape, abuse, divorce, unplanned pregnancy, surrender of a child for adoption—none of these painful experiences make us invisible to God or unable to serve him. And our Christian communities should be places where these stories can be heard.

Question 9. If your group includes a few folks with up-and-down life stories, spend time with those stories here if they would like to tell them. Don't push for "it's all okay now" statements; the person may still be deep in pain and unable to see a Romans 8:28 resolution as yet. However, the wells of God's provision, when they are recognized, should be warmly affirmed and celebrated.

Study 9. Receiving Life with Thanksgiving. 1 Timothy 4:1—5:2.

Purpose: To listen in as a wise single man counsels a younger man regarding such things as the goodness of life in the physical body, taking care of ourselves while we nurture others and rooting ourselves in church-family relationships.

Question 1. Whether Paul was actually the author of 1-2 Timothy and Titus was debated among scholars in the nineteenth and twentieth centuries because of vocabulary and style that mark these off from other of Paul's letters and because these "Pastoral Epistles" show much more attention to church organization. However, many careful biblical scholars today believe that the early church was right in accepting Paul's authorship. For a summary of the arguments, see E. Earle Ellis, "Pastoral Letters," in *Dictionary of Paul and His Letters*, ed. Gerald F. Hawthorne, Ralph P. Martin and Daniel G. Reid (Downers Grove, Ill.: InterVarsity Press, 1993), pp. 658-60.

Question 2. The issues here can be rather complex. In some ways today's evangelical churches are still under the influence of gnosticism, an early heresy based on the Platonic teaching that spirit is good and body/matter is bad. These influences underlie our mistrust of the arts (particularly painting, sculpture and dance), our abuse of the earth, our sometimes absurd debates over whether we are called to feed the hungry or "just preach the gospel." We mistrust beauty and pleasure and don't know how to deal with them theologically. Paradoxically (and this was also true of the earliest gnosticism), the notion that the physical really doesn't matter opens the way to gross physical self-indulgence—in contemporary Western Christian cultures, closets bulging with clothes, overeating, shopping as a hobby, expensively decorated homes, luxury cars.

Question 4. See verse 3. Paul may well be referring to such prohibitions here.

Question 5. Our residual gnosticism conditions us to assume verse 8 is teaching that "body is minimally okay, but spirit is *really* what matters." Resist the temptation! Given what Paul has said in verses 1-5, we can gather that godliness means receiving *all* of God's creation—food, sexuality, sleep, stars, animals, friendship, marriage, relationship with God, forgiveness, miracles, love—prayerfully and thankfully. Godliness is being a whole person in humble relationship with God.

Question 9. Because we don't have spouses to watch out for us and keep us grounded, we singles need to watch out for each other as Paul is doing for Timothy here. Paul isn't saying "Indulge yourself"—that would be completely out of character for someone who worked so sacrificially in lifelong mission—but "Remember who you are, how much God loves you; live out of your gifts and calling. Don't let others hold you back from your ministry or trick you. Be a godly person, a whole person, receiving God's good gifts."

Question 10. Ask group members to be specific—for example, "Cut back the TV watching; it is deadening you," or "Do you realize how much your niece looks up to you? You should take seriously your role in her life."

Study 10. Enlarging Your Tent. Isaiah 54.

Purpose: To appreciate the legacy we can give the world, and to gain boldness to live larger lives.

Group discussion. Help the group be very welcoming of each other's diversity in this regard. Some may not be able to afford an apartment much larger than a closet; some may own a beautiful house but be too busy to spend much time in it; some (particularly those from immigrant families) may live with parents and siblings; some, like Jesus and Paul, may live in deliberate transience out of faithfulness to their calling. The point is to begin thinking about whether we are simply marking time or investing ourselves in life for the long haul.

Question 1. Turning back to Isaiah 52:1-2 helps clarify that this is part of a longer prophetic poem addressed to Zion/Jerusalem; the imagery returns to a city's walls in 54:11-12. "Zion is a symbol or metaphor for the historical city of Jerusalem," associated with concepts such as "the covenant people of God" and "the renewed heavens and earth, from which peace and prosperity will reign" ("Zion," in *Dictionary of Biblical Imagery*, ed. Leland Ryken, James C. Wilhoit and Tremper Longman III [Downers Grove, Ill.: InterVarsity Press, 1998], p. 980). In Galatians 4:26-27 Paul quotes Isaiah 54:1 and exults, "The Jerusalem that is above [in contrast to the domain of religious law] is free, and she is our mother." He thus gives us permission to apply this passage to ourselves!

Question 2. Men, especially those who are less intuitive, may have a hard time with this image. They may need to return to the notion of *legacy*—knowing that one's life has permanent value, that there are others to nurture in the present who will inherit one's gifts in the future. It may also be helpful for participants to remember that in the ancient Near East infertility was seen as shameful, a divine curse—rather like the way singleness is still treated in some circles today.

Question 3. "The desolate woman" will have more children than the happily married woman. Isaiah is picturing a glorious restoration for Zion: after a tragic military defeat and period of exile, the devastated land will overflow with inhabitants. The image of triumphant reversal recalls Jesus' saying "Indeed there are many who are last who will be first, and first who will be last" (Lk 13:30).

Question 5. Some may notice that verse 4 alludes to widowhood while verses 6-8 picture abandonment and divorce. Remember, the prophet is piling up verbal images to picture what has happened and will happen to God's people. It is not actual widowhood, nor is it actual divorce—but it *feels like* both of these things.

Isaiah earlier warned God's people of coming national exile; chapter 54 is part of his vivid portrait of the ultimate restoration that will follow.

Question 6. Notice "husband," "the Lord Almighty," "Redeemer" and "God of the earth" (v. 5). "Redeemer" is not as large a jump from "husband" as we might initially think. Remember the book of Ruth, where Ruth invites Boaz to serve as her kinsman-redeemer and marry her (Ruth 3:1-13).

Question 9. Verse 9 is an allusion to Genesis 9, where God establishes a covenant with Noah's family "and with every living creature on earth" (Gen 9:10): never again will "the waters become a flood to destroy all life" (v. 15). In Isaiah 54:9-10 God uses the same "never again" language.

If the allusions to God's anger are troubling to group members, you may want to help them think of times when *human* love is expressed in anger. A mother is properly enraged when her child is abused—we would consider her sick or morally deficient if she weren't. After the terrorist attacks of September 11, 2001, Americans were reassured to hear their president and other leaders express profound anger. God's anger is like that: passion against evil, on behalf of evil's victims. It is grounded in God's goodness and love, not twisted as human anger often is.

Yet here God says that the time of his anger has passed. The prophet envisions a time of utter well-being, when God no longer has any occasion for righteous wrath.

Question 11. Jesus still says to his disciples, "I am the vine; you are the branches. If you remain in me and I in you, you will bear much fruit; apart from me you can do nothing. . . . You did not choose me, but I chose you and appointed you to go and bear fruit—fruit that will last" (Jn 15:5, 16).

Question 12. The group will do well to think of this in both individual and corporate terms. Perhaps they should consider how together they can reach out to people in need rather than focusing entirely on self-nurture.

Ruth Goring is a campus minister at the College of DuPage and senior copyeditor at InterVarsity Press. Poet, essayist and mother of two, she is also the author of Meeting God in Relationships *and* Meeting God in Quiet.

What Should We Study Next?

A good place to continue your study of Scripture would be with a book study. Many groups begin with a Gospel such as *Mark* (20 studies by Jim Hoover) or *John* (26 studies by Douglas Connelly). These guides are divided into two parts so that if twenty or twenty-six weeks seems like too much to do at once, the group can feel free to do half and take a break with another topic. Later you might want to come back to it. You might prefer to try a shorter letter. *Philippians* (9 studies by Donald Baker), *Ephesians* (11 studies by Andrew T. and Phyllis J. Le Peau) and *1 & 2 Timothy and Titus* (11 studies by Pete Sommer) are good options. If you want to vary your reading with an Old Testament book, consider *Ecclesiastes* (12 studies by Bill and Teresa Syrios) for a challenging and exciting study.

There are a number of interesting topical LifeGuide studies as well. Here are some options for filling three or four quarters of a year:

Basic Discipleship
Christian Beliefs, 12 studies by Stephen D. Eyre
Christian Character, 12 studies by Andrea Sterk & Peter Scazzero
Christian Disciplines, 12 studies by Andrea Sterk & Peter Scazzero
Evangelism, 12 studies by Rebecca Pippert & Ruth Siemens

Building Community
Christian Community, 10 studies by Rob Suggs
Fruit of the Spirit, 9 studies by Hazel Offner
Spiritual Gifts, 12 studies by Charles & Anne Hummel

Character Studies
David, 12 studies by Jack Kuhatschek
New Testament Characters, 12 studies by Carolyn Nystrom
Old Testament Characters, 12 studies by Peter Scazzero
Women of the Old Testament, 12 studies by Gladys Hunt

The Trinity
Meeting God, 12 studies by J. I. Packer
Meeting Jesus, 13 studies by Leighton Ford
Meeting the Spirit, 12 studies by Douglas Connelly